Buckdancer's Choice

Buckdancer's Choice

Poems by JAMES DICKEY

WESLEYAN UNIVERSITY PRESS, *Middletown, Connecticut*

Acknowledgment is gratefully made to the following magazines in which these poems first appeared: *The Bulletin; Harper's; The Hudson Review; The Kenyon Review; Partisan Review; Quarterly Review of Literature; The Southern Review; Virginia Quarterly Review; Poetry: A Magazine of Verse,* which published "The Firebombing"; and *The New Yorker,* which published "Angina," "The Aura," "Buckdancer's Choice," "The Common Grave," "The Escape," "Reincarnation," "The Shark's Parlor," "Them, Crying," "The War Wound," and a slightly shorter version of "Slave Quarters."

Library of Congress Catalog Number: 65-21079

Manufactured in the United States of America

First printing September 1965; second printing March 1966; third printing May 1966; fourth printing August 1966.

To Maibelle Swift Dickey

and

Eugene Dickey

life-givers

Contents

Buckdancer's Choice

Part 1

The Firebombing

Denke daran, dass nach den grossen Zerstörungen
Jedermann beweisen wird, dass er unschuldig war.
—Günter Eich

Or hast thou an arm like God?
—The Book of Job

Homeowners unite.

All families lie together, though some are burned alive.
The others try to feel
For them. Some can, it is often said.

Starve and take off

Twenty years in the suburbs, and the palm trees willingly leap
Into the flashlights,
And there is beneath them also
A booted crackling of snailshells and coral sticks.
There are cowl flaps and the tilt cross of propellers,
The shovel-marked clouds' far sides against the moon,
The enemy filling up the hills
With ceremonial graves. At my somewhere among these,

Snap, a bulb is tricked on in the cockpit

And some technical-minded stranger with my hands
Is sitting in a glass treasure-hole of blue light,
Having potential fire under the undeodorized arms

11

Of his wings, on thin bomb-shackles,
The "tear-drop-shaped" 300-gallon drop-tanks
Filled with napalm and gasoline.

Thinking forward ten minutes
From that, there is also the burst straight out
Of the overcast into the moon; there is now
The moon-metal-shine of propellers, the quarter-
moonstone, aimed at the waves,
Stopped on the cumulus.

There is then this re-entry
Into cloud, for the engines to ponder their sound.
In white dark the aircraft shrinks; Japan

Dilates around it like a thought.
Coming out, the one who is here is over
Land, passing over the all-night grainfields,
In dark paint over
The woods with one silver side,
Rice-water calm at all levels
Of the terraced hill.
                Enemy rivers and trees
Sliding off me like snakeskin,
Strips of vapor spooled from the wingtips
Going   invisible   passing   over   on
Over   bridges   roads for nightwalkers
Sunday night in the enemy's country   absolute
Calm   the moon's face   coming   slowly
About
        the inland sea
Slants   is woven with wire thread
Levels out   holds together like a quilt
Off the starboard wing   cloud flickers

12

At my glassed-off forehead   the moon's now and again
Uninterrupted face going forward
Over the waves in a glide-path
Lost into land.

Going: going with it

Combat booze by my side in a cratered canteen,
Bourbon frighteningly mixed
With GI pineapple juice,
Dogs trembling under me for hundreds of miles, on many
Islands, sleep-smelling that ungodly mixture
Of napalm and high-octane fuel,
Good bourbon and GI juice.

Rivers circling behind me around
Come to the fore, and bring
A town with everyone darkened.
Five thousand people are sleeping off
An all-day American drone.
Twenty years in the suburbs have not shown me
Which ones were hit and which not.

Haul on the wheel   racking slowly
The aircraft blackly around
In a dark dream   that   that is
That is like flying inside someone's head

Think of this   think of this

I did not think of my house
But think of my house now

Where the lawn mower rests on its laurels
Where the diet exists

For my own good   where I try to drop
Twenty years, eating figs in the pantry
Blinded by each and all
Of the eye-catching cans that gladly have caught my wife's eye
Until I cannot say
Where the screwdriver is   where the children
Get off the bus   where the new
Scoutmaster lives   where the fly
Hones his front legs   where the hammock folds
Its erotic daydreams   where the Sunday
School text for the day has been put   where the fire
Wood is   where the payments
For everything under the sun
Pile peacefully up,

But in this half-paid-for pantry
Among the red lids that screw off
With an easy half-twist to the left
And the long drawers crammed with dim spoons,
I still have charge — secret charge —
Of the fire developed to cling
To everything: to golf carts and fingernail
Scissors as yet unborn   tennis shoes
Grocery baskets   toy fire engines
New Buicks stalled by the half-moon
Shining at midnight on crossroads   green paint
Of jolly garden tools   red Christmas ribbons:

Not atoms, these, but glue inspired
By love of country to burn,
The apotheosis of gelatin.

Behind me having risen the Southern Cross
Set up by chaplains in the Ryukyus —

14

Orion, Scorpio, the immortal silver
Like the myths of king-
insects at swarming time —
One mosquito, dead drunk
On altitude, drones on, far under the engines,
And bites between
The oxygen mask and the eye.
The enemy-colored skin of families
Determines to hold its color
In sleep, as my hand turns whiter
Than ever, clutching the toggle —
The ship shakes   bucks
Fire hangs   not yet fire
In the air above Beppu
For I am fulfilling

An "anti-morale" raid upon it.
All leashes of dogs
Break under the first bomb, around those
In bed, or late in the public baths: around those
Who inch forward on their hands
Into medicinal waters.
Their heads come up with a roar
Of Chicago fire:
Come up with the carp pond showing
The bathhouse upside down,
Standing stiller to show it more
As I sail artistically over
The resort town followed by farms,
Singing and twisting
All the handles in heaven   kicking
The small cattle off their feet
In a red costly blast
Flinging jelly over the walls

15

As in a chemical war-
fare field demonstration.
With fire of mine like a cat

Holding onto another man's walls,
My hat should crawl on my head
In streetcars, thinking of it,
The fat on my body should pale.

Gun down
The engines, the eight blades sighing
For the moment when the roofs will connect
Their flames, and make a town burning with all
American fire.
                    Reflections of houses catch;
Fire shuttles from pond to pond
In every direction, till hundreds flash with one death.
With this in the dark of the mind,
Death will not be what it should;
Will not, even now, even when
My exhaled face in the mirror
Of bars, dilates in a cloud like Japan.
The death of children is ponds
Shutter-flashing; responding mirrors; it climbs
The terraces of hills
Smaller and smaller, a mote of red dust
At a hundred feet; at a hundred and one it goes out.
That is what should have got in
To my eye

And shown the insides of houses, the low tables
Catch fire from the floor mats,
Blaze up in gas around their heads
Like a dream of suddenly growing

16

Too intense for war. Ah, under one's dark arms
Something strange-scented falls—when those on earth
Die, there is not even sound;
One is cool and enthralled in the cockpit,
Turned blue by the power of beauty,
In a pale treasure-hole of soft light
Deep in aesthetic contemplation,
Seeing the ponds catch fire
And cast it through ring after ring
Of land: O death in the middle
Of acres of inch-deep water!   Useless

Firing   small arms
Speckles   from the river
Bank   one ninety-millimeter
Misses   far down   wrong petals   gone

It is this detachment,
The honored aesthetic evil,
The greatest sense of power in one's life,
That must be shed in bars, or by whatever
Means, by starvation
Visions in well-stocked pantries:
The moment when the moon sails in between
The tail-booms   the rudders nod   I swing
Over   directly over the heart
The *heart* of the fire. A mosquito burns out on my cheek
With the cold of my face   there are the eyes
In blue light   bar light
All masked but them   the moon
Crossing from left to right   in the streams below
Oriental fish form quickly
In the chemical shine,
In their eyes one tiny seed

17

Of deranged, Old Testament light.

Letting go   letting go
The plane rises gently   dark forms
Glide off me   long water   pales
In safe zones   a new cry enters
The voice box of chained family dogs

We buck   leap over something
Not there   settle back
Leave it   leave it clinging and crying
It consumes them in a hot
Body-flash, old age or menopause
Of children, clings and burns
                              eating through
And when a reed mat catches fire
From me, it explodes through field after field
Bearing its sleeper   another

Bomb finds a home
And clings to it like a child. And so

Goodbye to the grassy mountains
To cloud streaming from the night engines
Flags   pennons   curved silks
Of air   myself streaming also
My body covered
With flags, the air of flags
Between the engines.
Forever I do sleep in that position,
Forever in a turn
For home that breaks out streaming banners
From my wingtips,
Wholly in position to admire.

18

O then I knock it off
And turn for home over the black complex thread worked through
The silver night-sea,
Following the huge, moon-washed steppingstones
Of the Ryukyus south,
The nightgrass of mountains billowing softly
In my rising heat.
                              Turn and tread down
The yellow stones of the islands
To where Okinawa burns,
Pure gold, on the radar screen,
Beholding, beneath, the actual island form
In the vast water-silver poured just above solid ground,
An inch of water extending for thousands of miles
Above flat ploughland. Say "down," and it is done.

All this, and I am still hungry,
Still twenty years overweight, still unable
To get down there or see
What really happened.
                              But it may be that I could not,
If I tried, say to any
Who lived there, deep in my flames: say, in cold
Grinning sweat, as to another
As these homeowners who are always curving
Near me down the different-grassed street: say
As though to the neighbor
I borrowed the hedge-clippers from
On the darker-grassed side of the two,
Come in, my house is yours, come in
If you can, if you
Can pass this unfired door. It is that I can imagine
At the threshold nothing
With its ears crackling off

Like powdery leaves,
Nothing with children of ashes, nothing not
Amiable, gentle, well-meaning,
A little nervous for no
Reason   a little worried   a little too loud
Or too easygoing   nothing I haven't lived with
For twenty years, still nothing not as
American as I am, and proud of it.

Absolution? Sentence? No matter;
The thing itself is in that.

Part 2

Buckdancer's Choice

So I would hear out those lungs,
The air split into nine levels,
Some gift of tongues of the whistler

In the invalid's bed: my mother,
Warbling all day to herself
The thousand variations of one song;

It is called Buckdancer's Choice.
For years, they have all been dying
Out, the classic buck-and-wing men

Of traveling minstrel shows;
With them also an old woman
Was dying of breathless angina,

Yet still found breath enough
To whistle up in my head
A sight like a one-man band,

Freed black, with cymbals at heel,
An ex-slave who thrivingly danced
To the ring of his own clashing light

Through the thousand variations of one song
All day to my mother's prone music,
The invalid's warbler's note,

While I crept close to the wall
Sock-footed, to hear the sounds alter,
Her tongue like a mockingbird's break

Through stratum after stratum of a tone
Proclaiming what choices there are
For the last dancers of their kind,

For ill women and for all slaves
Of death, and children enchanted at walls
With a brass-beating glow underfoot,

Not dancing but nearly risen
Through barnlike, theatrelike houses
On the wings of the buck and wing.

Faces Seen Once

Faces seen once are seen

To fade from around one feature,
Leaving a chin, a scar, an expression

Forever in the air beneath a streetlight,
Glancing in boredom from the window
Of a bus in a country town,
Showing teeth for a moment only,
All of which die out of mind, except
One silver one.

Who had the dog-bitten ear?
The granulated lids? The birthmark?

Faces seen once change always

Into and out of each other:
An eye you saw in Toulon
Is gazing at you down a tin drainpipe
You played with as a dull child
In Robertstown, Georgia.
There it is April; the one eye

Concentrates, the rusty pipe

Is trembling; behind the eye
Is a pine tree blurring with tears:

You and someone's blue eye
Transforming your boyhood are weeping
For an only son drowned in warm water

23

With the French fleet off Senegal.
Soon after, the cancer-clamped face
Of your great-grandfather relaxes,

Smiles again with the lips of a newsboy.
Faces seen once make up

One face being organized

And changed and known less all the time,
Unsexed, amorphous, growing in necessity
As you deepen in age.
The brow wrinkles, a blind, all-knowing
Questioning look comes over it,
And every face in the street begins

To partake of the look in the eyes,

Every nose is part of that nose
And changes the nose; every innocence and every

Unspoken-of guilt goes into it,
Into the face of the one
Encountered, unknowable person who waits
For you all over the world,
In coffee shops, filling stations, bars,
In mills and orphan asylums,

In hospitals, prisons, at parties,
Yearning to be one thing.

At your death, they — it is there,

And the features congeal,
Having taken the last visage in,
Over you, pretesting its smile,
The skin the indwelling no
Color of all colors mingled,
The eyes asking all there is.

Composed, your own face trembles near

Joining that other, knowing
That finally something must break

Or speak. A silver tooth gleams;
You mumble, whispering "You
Are human, are what I have witnessed.
You are all faces seen once."
Through the bent, staring, unstable dark
Of a drainpipe, Unity hears you —

A God-roar of hearing — say only
"You are an angel's too-realized

Unbearable memoryless face."

The Common Grave

I

Some sit and stare
In an unknown direction, though most lie still,
Knowing that every season
Must be wintered.

II

The mover of mists and streams
Is usually in the weeds
By twilight, taking slowly
A dark dedicated field-shape.

III

Of all those who are under,
Many are looking over
Their shoulder, although it is only one leap
To beyond-reason gold, only one
Breath to the sun's great city.
All ages of mankind unite
Where it is dark enough.

IV

The midstrides of out-of-shape runners,
The discarded strokes of bad swimmers,
Open-mouthed at the wrong time—
All these are hooked wrongly together.
A rumor runs through them like roots:
They must try even harder

To bring into their vast,
Indiscriminate embrace
All of humanity.

V

In someone's hand an acorn
Pulses, thinking
It is only one leap,
Only one.

VI

In the field by twilight are
The faller in leaves through October,
The white-headed flyer in thistles
Finding out secret currents of air,
The raiser of mists from the creekbed,
A fish extending his body
Through all the curves of the river,
The incredible moon in the voice box
Of dogs on All Souls' Night.

VII

All creatures tumbled together
Get back in their wildest arms
No single thing but each other,
Hear only sounds like train sounds,
Cattle sounds, earth-shakers.

VIII

The mover of all things struggles

In the green-crowded, green-crowned nightmare
Of a great king packed in an acorn.
A train bends round a curve
Like a fish. An oak tree breaks
Out and shoves for the moonlight,
Bearing leaves which shall murmur for years,
Dumfoundedly, like mouths opened all at once
At just the wrong time to be heard,
    Others, others.

Reincarnation

Still, passed through the spokes of an old wheel, on and around
The hub's furry rust in the weeds and shadows of the riverbank,
This one is feeling his life as a man move slowly away.
Fallen from that estate, he has gone down on his knees
And beyond, disappearing into the egg buried under the sand

And wakened to the low world being born, consisting now
Of the wheel on its side not turning, but leaning to rot away
In the sun a few feet farther off than it is for any man.
The roots bulge quietly under the earth beneath him;
With his tongue he can hear them in their concerted effort

To raise something, anything, out of the dark of the ground.
He has come by gliding, by inserting the head between stems.
Everything follows that as naturally as the creation
Of the world, leaving behind arms and legs, leaving behind
The intervals between tracks, leaving one long wavering step

In sand and none in grass: he moves through, moving nothing,
And the grass stands as never entered. It is in the new
Life of resurrection that one can come in one's own time
To a place like a rotting wheel, the white paint flaking from it,
Rust slowly emerging, and coil halfway through it, stopped

By a just administration of light and dark over the diamonds
Of the body. Here, also naturally growing, is a flat leaf
To rest the new head upon. The stem bends but knows the weight
And does not touch the ground, holding the snub, patterned face
Swaying with the roots of things. Inside the jaws, saliva

Has turned ice cold, drawn from bird eggs and thunderstruck rodents,
Dusty pine needles, blunt stones, horse dung, leaf mold,

29

But mainly, now, from waiting—all the time a symbol of evil—
Not for food, but for the first man to walk by the gentle river:
Minute by minute the head becomes more poisonous and poised.

Here in the wheel is the place to wait, with the eyes unclosable,
Unanswerable, the tongue occasionally listening, this time
No place in the body desiring to burn the tail away or to warn,
But only to pass on, handless, what yet may be transferred
In a sudden giving-withdrawing move, like a county judge striking a
    match.

Them, Crying

In the well-fed cage-sound of diesels,
Here, in the cab's boxed wind,
He is called to by something beyond
His life. In the sun's long haul
Of light, each week at this place,
He sings to the truck's eight wheels

But at night it is worse than useless:
The great building shoots and holds

Its rays, and he hears, through the engine,
Through the killed words of his own song,
Them: them crying. Unmarried, unchildlike,
Half-bearded and foul-mouthed, he feels
His hands lean away to the right
And bear the truck spiraling down

To the four streets going around
And around and around the hospital.

He sits, and the voices are louder,
An awakening, part-song sound
Calling anyone out of the life
He thought he led: a sound less than twelve
Years old, which wakes to the less-than-nothing
Of a bent glass straw in a glass

With small sleepless bubbles stuck to it:
Which feels a new mouth sewn shut

In a small body's back or its side
And would free some angelic voice

From the black crimped thread,
The snipped cat-whiskers of a wound—
A sound that can find no way
To attack the huge, orderly flowers.

At one-thirty he is drawn in,
Drawn in, drawn in and in,

Listening, through dozens of Bakelite floors
And walls, brogan-stepping along
Through green-tiled nightlighted rooms
Where implements bake in glass cases,
Through halls full of cloudy test tubes,
Up and down self-service elevators

That open both sides at once,
Through closets of lubricants,

Through a black beehive of typed labels,
Through intimate theatres
Scrubbed down with Lysol and salt,
Through a sordid district of pails,
Until, on the third floor rear
Of the donated Southeast Wing,

He comes on a man holding wrongly
A doll with feigning-closed eyes,

And a fat woman, hat in her lap,
Has crashed through a chairback to sleep.
Unbelonging, he circles their circle;
Then, as though a stitch broke
In his stomach, he wheels and goes through
The double-frosted warning-marked door.

Twelve parents at bay intone
In the brain waves that wash around heroes:

Come, stripped to your T-shirt sleeves,
Your coveralls, blue jeans, or chains,
Your helmets or thickening haircuts,
Your white coats, your rock-pounding foreheads,
For our children lie there beyond us
In the still, foreign city of pain

Singing backward into the world
To those never seen before,

Old cool-handed doctors and young ones,
Capped girls bearing vessels of glucose,
Ginger ward boys, pan handlers, technicians,
Thieves, nightwalkers, truckers, and drunkards
Who must hear, not listening, them:
Them, crying: for they rise only unto

Those few who transcend themselves,
The superhuman tenderness of strangers.

The Celebration

All wheels; a man breathed fire,
Exhaling like a blowtorch down the road
And burnt the stripper's gown
Above her moving-barely feet.
A condemned train climbed from the earth
Up stilted nightlights zooming in a track.
I ambled along in that crowd

Between the gambling wheels
At carnival time with the others
Where the dodgem cars shuddered, sparking
On grillwire, each in his vehicle half
In control, half helplessly power-mad
As he was in the traffic that brought him.
No one blazed at me; then I saw

My mother and my father, he leaning
On a dog-chewed cane, she wrapped to the nose
In the fur of exhausted weasels.
I believed them buried miles back
In the country, in the faint sleep
Of the old, and had not thought to be
On this of all nights compelled

To follow where they led, not losing
Sight, with my heart enlarging whenever
I saw his crippled Stetson bob, saw her
With the teddy bear won on the waning
Whip of his right arm. They laughed;
She clung to him; then suddenly
The Wheel of wheels was turning

The colored night around.
They climbed aboard. My God, they rose
Above me, stopped themselves and swayed
Fifty feet up; he pointed
With his toothed cane, and took in
The whole Midway till they dropped,
Came down, went from me, came and went

Faster and faster, going up backward,
Cresting, out-topping, falling roundly.
From the crowd I watched them,
Their gold teeth flashing,
Until my eyes blurred with their riding
Lights, and I turned from the standing
To the moving mob, and went on:

Stepped upon sparking shocks
Of recognition when I saw my feet
Among the others, knowing them given,
Understanding the whirling impulse
From which I had been born,
The great gift of shaken lights,
The being wholly lifted with another,

All this having all and nothing
To do with me. Believers, I have seen
The wheel in the middle of the air
Where old age rises and laughs,
And on Lakewood Midway became
In five strides a kind of loving,
A mortal, a dutiful son.

The Escape

From my great-grandmother on,
My family lies at Fairmount
In a small rigid house of Tate marble.
A Civil War general, a small one,
Rises into the air,
Always fifty feet away,
And there are always flowers
Surrounding him as he lifts
His sword and calls back over his shoulder
To his troops, none of which lie
Under the decent plots and polished stones
Of the civilian dead. Once I saw,
Or said I did, a lily wrapped
Around his tense hand and sword hilt.
An enormous glass-fronted hospital
Rises across the street, the traffic
Roars equally from all four sides,
And often, from a textile mill,
A teen-age girl wanders by,
Her head in a singing cloth
Still humming with bobbins and looms.
In summer, the hospital orderlies eat
Their lunches on the lawn
From wet-spotted brown paper bags,
While behind them the portioned glass
Of the hospital blindingly fits
The noon sun together:
A tremendous vertical blaze
 From which one piece — off-center, northwest —
Is gone, where a window is open.

I have escaped from Fairmount
Through that square hole in the light,
Having found where that piece of the sun's
Stupendous puzzle resides. It is
Lying in the woods, in a small, unfenced
County graveyard in Alabama.
It is on an open book
Of cardboard and paper, a simulated Bible,
All white, like a giant bride's,
The only real pages the ones
The book opens to; light
From the trees is falling squarely
On the few large, hand-written words.
On a hunting trip I walked through
That place, far from all relatives
And wars, from bobbins and lilies and trucks.
Because of what I had seen,

I walked through the evergreen gates
Of the forest ranger's station,
And out to my car, and drove
To the county seat, and bought
My own secret grave-plot there
For thirty-seven dollars and a half.
A young deer, a spike buck, stood
Among the graves, slowly puzzling out
The not-quite-edible words
Of the book lying under
A panel of the sun forever
Missing from the noonlight of Fairmount.
I remember that, and sleep
Easier, seeing the animal head

Nuzzling the fragment of Scripture,
Browsing, before the first blotting rain
On the fragile book
Of the new dead, on words I take care,
Even in sleep, not to read,
Hoping for Genesis.

The Shark's Parlor

Memory: I can take my head and strike it on a wall   on Cumberland
    Island
Where the night tide came crawling under the stairs   came up the first
Two or three steps   and the cottage stood on poles all night
With the sea sprawled under it   as we dreamed of the great fin circling
Under the bedroom floor. In daylight there was my first brassy taste of
    beer
And Payton Ford and I came back from the Glynn County
    slaughterhouse
With a bucket of entrails and blood. We tied one end of a hawser
To a spindling porch pillar and rowed straight out of the house
Three hundred yards into the vast front yard of windless blue water
The rope outslithering its coil   the two-gallon jug stoppered and
    sealed
With wax   and a ten-foot chain leader   a drop-forged shark hook
    nestling.
We cast our blood on the waters   the land blood easily passing
For sea blood   and we sat in it for a moment with the stain spreading
Out from the boat   sat in a new radiance   in the pond of blood in
    the sea
Waiting for fins   waiting to spill our guts also in the glowing water.
We dumped the bucket, and baited the hook with a run-over collie
    pup. The jug
Bobbed, trying to shake off the sun as a dog would shake off the sea.
We rowed to the house   feeling the same water lift the boat a new way,
All the time seeing where we lived rise and dip with the oars.
We tied up and sat down in rocking chairs, one eye or the other
    responding
To the blue-eye wink of the jug. Payton got us a beer and we sat

All morning sat there with blood on our minds   the red mark out
In the harbor slowly failing us   then   the house groaned   the rope

Sprang out of the water   splinters flew   we leapt from our chairs
And grabbed the rope   hauled   did nothing   the house coming
     subtly
Apart   all around us   underfoot   boards beginning to sparkle
     like sand
With the glinting of the bright hidden parts of ten-year-old nails
Pulling out   the tarred poles we slept propped-up on   leaning to sea
As in land wind   crabs scuttling from under the floor   as we took
     turns about
Two more porch pillars   and looked out and saw   something
     a fish-flash
An almighty fin in trouble   a moiling of secret forces   a false start
Of water   a round wave growing: in the whole of Cumberland
     Sound the one ripple.
Payton took off without a word   I could not hold him either

But clung to the rope anyway: it was the whole house bending
Its nails that held whatever it was   coming in a little and like a fool
I took up the slack on my wrist. The rope drew gently   jerked   I lifted
Clean off the porch and hit the water   the same water it was in
I felt in blue blazing terror at the bottom of the stairs and scrambled
Back up looking desperately into the human house as deeply as I could
Stopping my gaze before it went out the wire screen of the back door
Stopped it on the thistled rattan   the rugs I lay on and read
On my mother's sewing basket with next winter's socks spilling from it
The flimsy vacation furniture   a bucktoothed picture of myself.
Payton came back with three men from a filling station   and glanced
     at me
Dripping water   inexplicable   then we all grabbed hold like a
     tug-of-war.

We were gaining a little   from us a cry went up   from everywhere
People came running. Behind us the house filled with men and boys.
On the third step from the sea I took my place   looking down the rope

40

Going into the ocean, humming and shaking off drops. A houseful
Of people put their backs into it   going up the steps from me
Into the living room   through the kitchen   down the back stairs
Up and over a hill of sand   across a dust road   and onto a raised
    field
Of dunes   we were gaining   the rope in my hands began to be wet
With deeper water   all other haulers retreated through the house
But Payton and I on the stairs   drawing hand over hand on our blood
Drawing into existence by the nose   a huge body   becoming
A hammerhead   rolling in beery shallows   and I began to let up
But the rope still strained behind me   the town had gone
Pulling-mad in our house: far away in a field of sand they struggled
They had turned their backs on the sea   bent double   some on
    their knees
The rope over their shoulders like a bag of gold   they strove for the
    ideal
Esso station across the scorched meadow   with the distant fish
    coming up
The front stairs   the sagging boards   still coming in   up   taking
Another step   toward the empty house   where the rope stood
    straining
By itself through the rooms   in the middle of the air. "Pass the word,"
Payton said, and I screamed it: "Let up, good God, let up!"   to no
    one there.
The shark flopped on the porch, grating with salt-sand   driving
    back in
The nails he had pulled out   coughing chunks of his formless blood.
The screen door banged and tore off   he scrambled on his tail   slid
Curved   did a thing from another world   and was out of his
    element and in
Our vacation paradise   cutting all four legs from under the dinner
    table
With one deep-water move   he unwove the rugs in a moment
    throwing pints

41

Of blood over everything we owned   knocked the buck teeth out of
     my picture
His odd head full of crushed jelly-glass splinters and radio tubes
     thrashing
Among the pages of fan magazines   all the movie stars drenched in
     sea-blood.
Each time we thought he was dead   he struggled back and smashed
One more thing   in all coming back to die   three or four more
     times after death.
At last we got him out   log-rolling him   greasing his sandpaper skin
With lard to slide him   pulling on his chained lips as the tide came
Tumbled him down the steps as the first night wave went under the
     floor.
He drifted off   head back   belly white as the moon. What could I
     do but buy
That house   for the one black mark still there   against death   a
     forehead-
toucher in the room he circles beneath   and has been invited to
     wreck?
Blood hard as iron on the wall   black with time   still bloodlike
Can be touched whenever the brow is drunk enough: all changes:
     Memory:
Something like three-dimensional dancing in the limbs   with age
Feeling more in two worlds than one   in all worlds the growing
     encounters.

Part 3

Pursuit from Under

Often, in these blue meadows,
I hear what passes for the bark of seals

And on August week ends the cold of a personal ice age
Comes up through my bare feet
Which are trying to walk like a boy's again
So that nothing on earth can have changed
On the ground where I was raised.

The dark grass here is like
The pads of mukluks going on and on

Because I once burned kerosene to read
Myself near the North Pole
In the journal of Arctic explorers
Found, years after death, preserved
In a tent, part of whose canvas they had eaten

Before the last entry.
All over my father's land

The seal holes sigh like an organ,
And one entry carries more terror
Than the blank page that signified death
In 1912, on the icecap.
It says that, under the ice,

43

The killer whale darts and distorts,
Cut down by the flawing glass

To a weasel's shadow,
And when, through his ceiling, he sees
Anything darker than snow
He falls away
To gather more and more force

From the iron depths of cold water,
His shadow dwindling

Almost to nothing at all, then charges
Straight up, looms up at the ice and smashes
Into it with his forehead
To splinter the roof, to isolate seal or man
On a drifting piece of the floe

Which he can overturn.
If you run, he will follow you

Under the frozen pane,
Turning as you do, zigzagging,
And at the most uncertain of your ground
Will shatter through, and lean,
And breathe frankly in your face

An enormous breath smelling of fish.
With the stale lungs staining your air

You know the unsaid recognition
Of which the explorers died:
They had been given an image

Of how the downed dead pursue us.
They knew, as they starved to death,

That not only in the snow
But in the family field

The small shadow moves,
And under bare feet in the summer:
That somewhere the turf will heave,
And the outraged breath of the dead,
So long held, will form

Unbreathably around the living.
The cows low oddly here

As I pass, a small bidden shape
Going with me, trembling like foxfire
Under my heels and their hooves.
I shall write this by kerosene,
Pitch a tent in the pasture, and starve.

Fox Blood

Blood blister over my thumb-moon
Rising, under clear still plastic
Still rising strongly, on the rise
Of unleashed dog-sounds: sound broke,
Log opened. Moon rose

Clear bright. Dark homeland
Peeled backward, scrambling its vines.
Stream showed, scent paled
In the spray of mountain-cold water.
The smell dogs followed

In the bush-thorns hung like a scarf,
The silver sharp creek
Cut; off yonder, fox feet
Went printing into the dark: *there,*
In the other wood,

The uncornered animal's, running
Is half floating off
Upon instinct. Sails spread, fox wings
Lift him alive over gullies,
Hair tips all over him lightly

Touched with the moon's red silver,
Back-hearing around
The stream of his body the tongue of hounds
Feather him. In his own animal sun
Made of human moonlight,

He flies like a bolt running home,
Whose passage kills the current in the river,

Whose track through the cornfield shakes
The symmetry from the rows.
Once shot, he dives through a bush

And disappears into air.
That is the bush my hand
Went deeply through as I followed.
Like a wild hammer blazed my right thumb
In the flashlight and moonlight

And dried to one drop
Of fox blood I nail-polished in,
That lopsided animal sun
Over the nearly buried
Or rising human half-moon,

My glassed skin halfmooning wrongly.
Between them, the logging road, the stopped
Stream, the disappearance into
The one bush's common, foreseen
Superhuman door:

All this where I nailed it,
With my wife's nailbrush, on my finger,
To keep, not under, but over
My thumb, a hammering day-and-night sign
Of that country.

Fathers and Sons

I. THE SECOND SLEEP

Curled, too much curled, he was sleeping

In a chair too small for him, a restless chair
That held no place for his arms;

In his sleep he grew legs to replace them

As his father liftingly strained
And carried him to the next room.

All the time he settled away

A gentle man looked upon him
And then walked out of the house

And started his evergreen car.

Terrific impact, none his,
Killed him three blocks to the north.

In his second sleep the boy heard

The reared-up tearing of metal
Where a glassed-in face leapt and broke,

But to him it was something else,

An animal clash, a shock of resolving antlers,
And slept on, deeper and deeper

Into the mating season.

The next room filled with women; his nostrils
Flared, his eyes grew wide

And shot with blood under eyelids.

Brow lowered in strife, he stamped
In the laurel thicket, a herd of does

Trembling around him. Into the rhododendron

His rival faded like rain.
He stared around wildly, head down.

In the undying green, they woke him.

II. THE AURA

He used to wake to him
With a sense of music coming
Along with a body in movement.
It swayed with the motion of a hip
Rolling into the bathroom,
And, lying in bed in the winter dark

49

Of fathers, he heard rock-and-roll
Closed off while water ran through it,
Then the door opening, music
Opening, strolling down the hall,
Bad music moving all over
The house, electric guitars that followed

Some body around. It was his son,
With his portable radio always
At his belt, leaning over, adjusting the dial
For disc jockeys. That would be
The Skimmers, and that the Last
Survivors, moaning afar in the kitchen,

Who moved when the living moved.
He could hear him coming
From far away, every dawn,
And now the sound still coming
From everywhere is grief,
Unstoppable. At the beginning

Of his teens, his last year
Of bicycles, the wild
Music, traveling through the suburbs
From junior high, was broken on the road.
But it leapt everywhere
Into odd places: from every angle

It does not cease to be heard, the aura
Surrounding his son. He cannot hear it early
In the morning, unless he turns on his radio
By the bed, or leaves it on all night,
But in supermarkets it comes
Forth from the walls; it glances

From plate glass in department stores,
And he moves within his boy's
Chosen sounds: in cars, theatres,
In filling stations, in beer joints
Where he sits as though in the next phase
His son would have lived, hearing voices

Giving prizes for naming of tunes, those stations
Never off the air. He sits still
Wherever he is, as though caught
With music on him, or as if he were
About to be given it somewhere
In the region of the stomach:

That sound is the same, and yet not—
There is too much steadiness in it: none
Is carried rightly, none wavers
With the motion of adolescent walking, none
Lumbers as it should. Still, it is there
In trios of girls, in fake folk singers

From Brooklyn, and he enters, anywhere,
His son's life without the waking-
to-it, the irreplaceable motion
Of a body. Bongoes. Steel
Guitars. A precious cheapness
He would have grown out of. Something. Music.

Sled Burial, Dream Ceremony

While the south rains, the north
Is snowing, and the dead southerner
Is taken there. He lies with the top of his casket
Open, his hair combed, the particles in the air
Changing to other things. The train stops

In a small furry village, and men in flap-eared caps
And others with women's scarves tied around their heads
And business hats over those, unload him,
And one of them reaches inside the coffin and places
The southerner's hand at the center

Of his dead breast. They load him onto a sled,
An old-fashioned sled with high-curled runners,
Drawn by horses with bells, and begin
To walk out of town, past dull red barns
Inching closer to the road as it snows

Harder, past an army of gunny-sacked bushes,
Past horses with flakes in the hollows of their sway-backs,
Past round faces drawn by children
On kitchen windows, all shedding basic-shaped tears.
The coffin top still is wide open;

His dead eyes stare through his lids,
Not fooled that the snow is cotton. The woods fall
Slowly off all of them, until they are walking
Between rigid little houses of ice-fishers
On a plain which is a great plain of water

Until the last rabbit track fails, and they are
At the center. They take axes, shovels, mattocks,

Dig the snow away, and saw the ice in the form
Of his coffin, lifting the slab like a door
Without hinges. The snow creaks under the sled

As they unload him like hay, holding his weight by ropes.
Sensing an unwanted freedom, a fish
Slides by, under the hole leading up through the snow
To nothing, and is gone. The coffin's shadow
Is white, and they stand there, gunny-sacked bushes,

Summoned from village sleep into someone else's dream
Of death, and let him down, still seeing the flakes in the air
At the place they are born of pure shadow
Like his dead eyelids, rocking for a moment like a boat
On utter foreignness, before he fills and sails down.

Gamecock

Fear, jealousy and murder are the same
When they put on their long reddish feathers,
Their shawl neck and moccasin head
In a tree bearing levels of women.
There is yet no thread

Of light, and his scabbed feet tighten,
Holding sleep as though it were lockjaw,
His feathers damp, his eyes crazed
And cracked like the eyes
Of a chicken head cut off or wrung-necked

While he waits for the sun's only cry
All night building up in his throat
To leap out and turn the day red,
To tumble his hens from the pine tree,
And then will go down, his hackles

Up, looking everywhere for the other
Cock who could not be there,
Head ruffed and sullenly stepping
As upon his best human-curved steel:
He is like any fierce

Old man in a terminal ward:
There is the same look of waiting
That the sun prepares itself for;
The enraged, surviving-
another-day blood,

And from him at dawn comes the same
Cry that the world cannot stop.

In all the great building's blue windows
The sun gains strength; on all floors, women
Awaken—wives, nurses, sisters and daughters—

And he lies back, his eyes filmed, unappeased,
As all of them, clucking, pillow-patting,
Come to help his best savagery blaze, doomed, dead-
game, demanding, unreasonably
Battling to the death for what is his.

The Night Pool

There is this other element that shines
At night near human dwellings, glows like wool
From the sides of itself, far down:

From the deep end of heated water
I am moving toward her, first swimming,
Then touching my light feet to the floor,

Rising like steam from the surface
To take her in my arms, beneath the one window
Still giving off unsleeping light.

There is this other element, it being late
Enough, and in it I lift her, and can carry
Her over any threshold in the world,

Into any of these houses, apartments,
Her shoulders streaming, or above them
Into the mythical palaces. Her body lies

In my arms like a child's, not drowned,
Not drowned, and I float with her off
My feet. We are here; we move differently,

Sustained, closer together, not weighing
On ourselves or on each other, not near fish
Or anything but light, the one human light

From above that we lie in, breathing
Its precious abandoned gold. We rise out
Into our frozen land-bodies, and her lips

Turn blue, sealed against me. What I can do
In the unforgivable cold, in the least
Sustaining of all brute worlds, is to say

Nothing, not ask forgiveness, but only
Give her all that in my condition
I own, wrap her in many towels.

The War Wound

It wounded well—one time and
A half: once with instant blood and again
Reinfecting blackly, years later. Now all
    Is calm at the heel of my hand

    Where I grabbed, in a bellied-
in airplane, and caught the dark glass
Offered once in a lifetime by
    The brittle tachometer.

    Moons by the thousands
Have risen in all that time; I hold
The healed half-moon of that night.
    I tell it to shine as still

    As it can in the temperate flesh
That never since has balled into a fist,
To hover on nylon guitar strings
    Like the folk-moon itself;

    I tell it to burn like a poison
When my two children threaten themselves,
Wall-walking, or off the deep end
    Of a county swimming pool,

And with thousands of moons
Coming over me year after year,
I lie with it well under cover,
    The war of the millions,

Through glass ground under
Heel twenty-one years ago
Concentrating its light on my hand,
Small, but with world-fury.

Mangham

Somewhere between bells the right angles staggered
And Mangham poised, sensing thunder,
Something crooked in the straight lines of his brain.
Chalk dust rose from his shoulders, lost more
Weight, settled upward. The blackboard altered
Its screech, and the teeth of the children were set
On edge.

Above our doped heads the ceiling whitened
As the part in Mr. Mangham's hair
Lost its way; a gray lock fell;
Behind him as he turned, the Law
Of Cosines. He pressed the middle of his brow
With a handkerchief, looking at all of us
As he stepped

Quickly out of the room. In the center
Of the high school a sound arose from us,
A hive sound, amazing, increasing. I tore up my note
To Serena Hill, and leaned and spoke
Boldly to her in person. At the threshold
Mr. Mangham appeared with a handkerchief
Full of lumps;

He had raided the lunchroom icebox, and held
A knotted cloth full of soupy cubes
Dripping down his gray face: held it
Left-handed, lifted his good
Right arm. The signs appeared again,
The blackboard filled
With crazy proofs,

Lines wavering on the powdery blackness,
The dark night of the adolescent mind,
Conceiving drunken constellations,
Equilateral triangles, others of thirty-
sixty-ninety degrees, traced by a seismograph,
All figures melting from the ice-
colors of his chalk.

It should be in a tent in the desert
That I remember Mangham's last day
In that class, for his cracked voice was speaking
Of perfection, sphere-music,
Through the stroke that blazed in his mind
As our hive toned down
And Pythagoras howled

For more ice: it should be in contemplative sand
Or in a corner that I ought to sit
On a high stool, Mangham's age now,
On my head a conical hat, a dunce cap
Covered with moons and stars and jagged bands
Of brain-lightning, the ceiling above me
White with the chalk motes

Of stars from my shoulders, the night blazoned
With the angles of galaxies forming
To a silent music's accords,
Proving once and for all that I have no head
For figures, but knowing that that did not stop
Mangham for one freezing minute
Of his death

From explaining for my own good, from the good
Side of his face, while the other

Mixed unfelt sweat and ice water, what I never
Could get to save my soul: those things that, once
Established, cannot be changed by angels,
Devils, lightning, ice or indifference:
Identities! Identities!

Angina

That one who is the dreamer lies mostly in her left arm,
Where the pain shows first,
Tuned in on the inmost heart,
Never escaping. On the blue, bodied mound of chenille,
That limb lies still.
Death in the heart must be calm,

Must not look suddenly, but catch the windowframed squirrel
In a mild blue corner
Of an eye staring straight at the ceiling
And hold him there.
Cornered also, the oak tree moves
All the ruffled green way toward itself

Around the squirrel thinking of the sun
As small boys and girls tiptoe in
Overawed by their own existence,
For courtly doctors long dead
Have told her that to bear children
Was to die, and they are the healthy issue

Of four of those. Oh, beside that room the oak leaves
Burn out their green in an instant, renew it all
From the roots when the wind stops.
All afternoon she dreams of letters
To disc jockeys, requesting the "old songs,"
The songs of the nineties, when she married, and caught

With her first child rheumatic fever.
Existence is family: sometime,
Inadequate ghosts round the bed,
But mostly voices, low voices of serious drunkards

Coming in with the night light on
And the pink radio turned down;

She hears them ruin themselves
On the rain-weeping wires, the bearing-everything poles,
Then dozes, not knowing sleeping from dying—
It is day. Limbs stiffen when the heart beats
Wrongly. Her left arm tingles,
The squirrel's eye blazes up, the telephone rings,

Her children and her children's children fail
In school, marriage, abstinence, business.
But when I think of love
With the best of myself—that odd power—
I think of riding, by chairlift,
Up a staircase burning with dust

In the afternoon sun slanted also
Like stairs without steps
To a room where an old woman lies
Who can stand on her own two feet
Only six strange hours every month:
Where such a still one lies smiling

And takes her appalling risks
In absolute calm, helped only by the most
Helplessly bad music in the world, where death,
A chastened, respectful presence
Forced by years of excessive quiet
To be stiller than wallpaper roses,

Waits, twined in the roses, saying slowly
To itself, as sprier and sprier
Generations of disc jockeys chatter,

I must be still and not worry,
Not worry, not worry, to hold
My peace, my poor place, my own.

Dust

Lying at home
Anywhere   it can change not only the color
But the shape of the finger that runs along it   leaving a trail
That disappears from the earth; nothing can follow
Where that hand has walked and withdrawn.
And I have lain in bed at home and watched

Through a haze
Of afternoon liquor   the sun come down through it
Dropping off at the window sill from which the dust has risen
With no voice   the voices of children   to spin
In a stunned silence   the individual motes
All with a shape apiece   wool fragments

Small segments
Of rope tricks   spirochetes boring into the very
Body of light   and if you move your hand through their air
They dip   weave   then assume in the altered brightness
The places they have had, and all
Their wandering. Wherever it is,

It rises;
The place stands up and whirls   as in valleys
Of Arizona   where the world-armies of dust gather in sleeping
Hordes. I have seen them walking
Nearly out of the world   on a crazed foot
Spinning the ground beneath them

Into chaos.
These are dust devils, and in that sunny room
With the shape of their motes unmassed   not given a desert
I have closed my eyes and changed them into forms

Of fire   the dying's vision
Of incandescent worms:

For moment
After moment have lain as though whirling
Toward myself from the grains of the earth   in a cone
Of sunlight   massing my forces
To live in time   drawn into a shape
Of dust   and in that place

A woman
Came from my spinning side. There we lay
And stared at the ceiling of our house   at the extra motes
That danced about the raising of our hands
Unable to get in-
to a human form at this time

But ready
For children we might raise and call our own,
Teach to sing   to sweep the sills   to lift their hands
And make the dust dance in the air
Like bodies: ready:
Ready, always, for the next.

The Fiend

He has only to pass by a tree   moodily walking   head down
A worried accountant   not with it   and he is swarming
He is gliding up the underside light of leaves   upfloating
In a seersucker suit   passing window after window of her building.
He finds her at last, chewing gum   talking on the telephone.
The wind sways him softly   comfortably sighing   she must bathe
Or sleep.   She gets up, and he follows her along the branch
Into another room.   She stands there for a moment   and the
      teddy bear
On the bed feels its guts spin as she takes it by the leg and tosses
It off.   She touches one button at her throat, and rigor mortis
Slithers into his pockets, making everything there — keys, pen
and secret love — stand up.   He brings from those depths the knife
And flicks it open   it glints on the moon one time   carries
Through the dead walls   making a wormy static on the TV screen.
He parts the swarm of gnats that live excitedly at this perilous level
Parts the rarified light high windows give out into inhabited trees
Opens his lower body to the moon.   This night the apartments are
      sinking

To ground level   burying their sleepers in the soil   burying all floors
But the one where a sullen shopgirl gets ready to take a shower,
Her hair in rigid curlers, and the rest.   When she gives up
Her aqua terry-cloth robe the wind quits in mid-tree   the birds
Freeze to their perches round his head   a purely human light
Comes out of a one-man oak   around her an energy field   she stands
Rooted   not turning to anything else   then begins to move like a saint
Her stressed nipples rising like things about to crawl off her   as he gets
A hold on himself.   With that clasp she changes   senses   something

Some breath through the fragile walls   some all-seeing eye
Of God   some touch that enfolds her body   some hand come up

out of roots
That carries her as she moves   swaying   at this rare height.
    She wraps
The curtain around her and streams.   The room fades.   Then coming
Forth magnificently   the window blurred from within   she moves
    in a cloud
Chamber   the tree in the oak currents sailing   in clear air keeping
    pace
With her white breathless closet—he sees her mistily part her lips
As if singing to him   come up from river-fog   almost hears her as if
She sang alone in a cloud   its warmed light streaming into his branches
Out through the gauze glass of the window.   She takes off her
    bathing cap
The tree with him ascending   himself and the birds all moving
In darkness together   sleep crumbling the bark in their claws.
By this time he holds in his awkward, subtle limbs the limbs

Of a hundred understanding trees.   He has learned what a plant is like
When it moves near a human habitation   moving closer the later it is
Unfurling its leaves near bedrooms   still keeping its wilderness life
Twigs covering his body with only one way out   for his eyes into
    inner light
Of a chosen window   living with them night after night   watching
Watching with them at times their favorite TV shows   learning—
Though now and then he hears a faint sound: gunshot, bombing,
Building-fall—how to read lips: the lips of laconic cowboys
Bank robbers   old and young doctors tense-faced   gesturing savagely
In wards and corridors   like reading the lips of the dead

The lips of men interrupting the program at the wrong time
To sell you a good used car on the Night Owl Show   men silently
    reporting
The news out the window.   But the living as well, three-dimensioned,
Silent as the small gray dead, must sleep at last   must save their lives

By taking off their clothes. It is his beholding that saves them:
God help the dweller in windowless basements   the one obsessed
With drawing curtains this night. At three o'clock in the morning
He descends   a medium-sized shadow   while that one sleeps and turns
In her high bed in loss   as he goes limb by limb   quietly down
The trunk with one lighted side. Ground upon which he could not explain
His presence he walks with toes uncurled from branches, his bird-movements
Dying hard. At the sidewalk he changes   gains weight   a solid citizen

Once more.   At apartments there is less danger from dogs, but he has
For those a super-quiet hand   a hand to calm sparrows and rivers,
And watchdogs in half-tended bushes lie with him watching their women
Undress   the dog's honest eyes and the man's the same pure beast's
Comprehending the same essentials. Not one of these beheld would ever give
Him a second look   but he gives them all a first look that goes
On and on   conferring immortality while it lasts   while the suburb's leaves
Hold still enough   while whatever dog he has with him holds its breath
Yet seems to thick-pant   impatient as he with the indifferent men
Drifting in and out of the rooms   or staying on, too tired to move
Reading the sports page   dozing   plainly unworthy   for what women want
Dwells in bushes and trees: what they want is to look outward,

To look with the light streaming into the April limbs   to stand straighter
While their husbands' lips dry out   feeling that something is there
That could dwell in no earthly house: that in poplar trees or beneath
The warped roundabout of the clothesline   in the sordid disorder

70

Of communal backyards   some being is there in the shrubs
Sitting comfortably on a child's striped rubber ball filled with rainwater
Muffling his glasses with a small studious hand against a sudden
Flash of houselight from within   or flash from himself   a needle's eye
Uncontrollable   blaze of uncompromised being. Ah, the lingerie
Hung in the bathroom! The domestic motions of single girls living
        together
A plump girl girding her loins against her moon-summoned blood:
In that moon he stands   the only male lit by it, covered with
        leaf-shapes.
He coughs, and the smallest root responds   and in his lust he is set
By the wind in motion. That movement can restore the green eyes
Of middle age   looking   renewed   through the qualified light
Not quite reaching him where he stands again on the usual branch
Of his oldest love   his tie not loosened   a plastic shield
In his breast pocket full of pencils and ballpoint pens given him by
        salesmen
His hat correctly placed to shade his eyes   a natural gambler's tilt
And in summer wears an eyeshade   a straw hat Caribbean style.
In some guise or other he is near them when they are weeping without
        sound
When the teen-age son has quit school   when the girl has broken up
With the basketball star   when the banker walks out on his wife.
He sees mothers counsel desperately with pulsing girls face down
On beds full of overstuffed beasts   sees men dress as women
In ante-bellum costumes with bonnets   sees doctors come, looking
        oddly
Like himself   though inside the houses   worming a medical arm
Up under the cringing covers   sees children put angrily to bed
Sees one told an invisible fairy story   with lips moving silently as his
Are also moving   the book's few pages bright. It will take years
But at last he will shed his leaves   burn his roots   give up
Invisibility   will step out   will make himself known to the one
He cannot see loosen her blouse   take off luxuriously   with lips

        71

Compressed against her mouth-stain   her dress   her stockings
Her magic underwear.   To that one he will come   up frustrated pines
Down alleys   through window blinds   blind windows   kitchen doors
On summer evenings. It will be something small that sets him off:
Perhaps a pair of lace pants on a clothesline   gradually losing
Water to the sun   filling out in the warm light with a well-rounded
Feminine wind as he watches   having spent so many sleepless nights
Because of her   because of her hand on a shade always coming down
In his face   not leaving even a shadow stripped naked upon the
    brown paper
Waiting for her now in a green outdated car with a final declaration
Of love   pretending to read   and when she comes and takes down
Her pants, he will casually follow her in   like a door-to-door salesman
The godlike movement of trees stiffening with him   the light
Of a hundred favored windows   gone wrong somewhere in his glasses
Where his knocked-off panama hat was   in his painfully vanishing
    hair.

Part 4

Slave Quarters

In the great place the great house is gone from   in the sun
Room, near the kitchen of air   I look across at low walls
Of slave quarters, and feel my imagining loins

Rise with the madness of Owners
To take off the Master's white clothes
And slide all the way into moonlight
Two hundred years old with this moon.
Let me go,

Ablaze with my old me-
scent, in moonlight made by the mind
From the dusk sun, in the yard where my dogs would smell
For once what I totally am,
Flaming up in their brains as the Master
They but dimly had sensed through my clothes:
Let me stand as though moving

At midnight, now at the instant of sundown
When the wind turns

From sea wind to land, and the marsh grass
Hovers, changing direction:
                              there was this house
That fell before I got out. I can pull
It over me where I stand, up from the earth,
Back out of the shells
Of the sea:

73

                    become with the change of this air
A coastal islander, proud of his grounds,
His dogs, his spinet
From Savannah, his pale daughters,
His war with the sawgrass, pushed back into
The sea it crawled from. Nearer dark, unseen,
I can begin to dance
Inside my gabardine suit
As though I had left my silk nightshirt

In the hall of mahogany, and crept
To slave quarters to live out
The secret legend of Owners. Ah, stand up,
Blond loins, another
Love is possible! My thin wife would be sleeping
Or would not mention my absence:

                                    the moonlight

On these rocks can be picked like cotton
By a crazed Owner dancing-mad
With the secret repossession of his body

Phosphorescent and mindless, shedding
Blond-headed shadow on the sand,
Hounds pressing in their sleep
Around him, smelling his footblood
On the strange ground that lies between skins
With the roof blowing off slave quarters
To let the moon in burning
The years away
In just that corner where crabgrass proves it lives
Outside of time.
Who seeks the other color of his body,

74

His loins giving off a frail light
On the dark lively shipwreck of grass   sees
Water live where
The half-moon touches,
The moon made whole in one wave
Very far from the silent piano   the copy of Walter Scott
Closed on its thin-papered battles
Where his daughter practiced, decorum preventing the one
Bead of sweat in all that lace   collected at her throat
From breaking and humanly running
Over Mozart's unmortal keys—

                              I come past
A sand crab pacing sideways   his eyes out
On stalks   the bug-eyed vision of fiddler
Crabs sneaking a light on the run
From the split moon   holding in it a white man stepping
Down the road of clamshells and cotton   his eyes out
On stems   the tops of the sugar
Cane soaring   the sawgrass walking:
                              I come past
The stale pools left
Over from high tide   where the crab in the night sand
Is basting himself with his claws   moving ripples outward
Feasting on brightness
                    and above
A gull also crabs slowly,
Tacks, jibes   then turning the corner
Of wind, receives himself like a brother
As he glides down upon his reflection:

My body has a color not yet freed:
In that ruined house let me throw
Obsessive gentility off;

75

Let Africa rise upon me like a man
Whose instincts are delivered from their chains
Where they lay close-packed and wide-eyed
In muslin sheets
As though in the miserly holding
Of too many breaths by one ship.   Now

Worked in silver   their work lies all
Around me   the fields dissolving
Into the sea   and   not on a horse
I stoop to the soil   working
Gathering   moving to the rhythm of a music
That has crossed the ocean in chains

In the grass the great singing void of slave

Labor about me   the moonlight bringing
Sweat out of my back as though   the sun
Changed skins upon me   some other
Man moving near me on horseback   whom I look in the eyes
Once a day:
            there in that corner

Her bed turned to grass. Unsheltered by these walls
The outside fields form slowly
Anew, in a kind of barrelling blowing,
Bend in all the right places   as faintly Michael rows
The boat ashore   his spiritual lungs
Entirely filling the sail.   How take on the guilt

Of slavers? How shudder like one who made
Money from buying a people
To work as ghosts
In this blowing solitude?

I only stand here upon shells   dressed poorly
For nakedness   poorly
For the dark wrecked hovel of rebirth

Picking my way in thought
To the black room
Where starlight blows off the roof
And the great beasts that died with the minds
Of the first slaves, stand at the door, asking
For death, asking to be
Forgotten: the sadness of elephants
The visionary pain in the heads
Of incredibly poisonous snakes
Lion   wildebeest   giraffe   all purchased also
When one wished only
Labor
          those beasts becoming
For the white man the animals of Eden
Emblems of sexual treasure   all beasts attending
Me now   my dreamed dogs snarling at the shades
Of eland and cheetah
On the dispossessed ground where I dance
In my clothes beyond movement:

In nine months she would lie
With a knife between her teeth to cut the pain
Of bearing
A child who belongs in no world   my hair in that boy
Turned black   my skin
Darkened by half   his, lightened
By that half exactly   the beasts of Africa reduced
To cave shadows flickering on his brow
As I think of him: a child would rise from that place
With half my skin.   He could for an instant

77

Of every day   when the wind turns   look
Me in the eyes.   What do you feel when passing

Your blood beyond death
To another in secret: into
Another who takes your features   and adds
A misplaced Africa to them,
Changing them forever
As they must live?   What happens
To you, when such a one bears
You after your death into rings
Of battling light   a heavyweight champion
Through the swirling glass of four doors,
In epauletted coats   into places
Where you learn to wait
On tables   into sitting in all-night cages
Of parking lots   into raising
A sun-sided spade in a gang
Of men on a tar road working
Until the crickets give up?
What happens when the sun goes down

And the white man's loins still stir
In a house of air   still draw him toward
Slave quarters? When Michael's voice is heard
Bending the sail like grass,
The real moon begins to come
Apart on the water
And two hundred years are turned back
On with the headlights of a car?
When you learn that there is no hatred
Like love in the eyes
Of a wholly owned face?   When you think of what
It would be like   what it has been

78

What it is to look once a day
Into an only
Son's brown, waiting, wholly possessed
Amazing eyes, and not
Acknowledge, but own?

THE WESLEYAN POETRY PROGRAM

Distinguished contemporary poetry in cloth and **paperback editions**

Alan Ansen: *Disorderly Houses* (1961)
John Ashbery: *The Tennis Court Oath* (1962)
Robert Bagg: *Madonna of the Cello* (1961)
Robert Bly: *Silence in the Snowy Fields* (1962)
Tram Combs: *st. thomas. poems.* (1965)
Donald Davie: *Events and Wisdoms* (1965)
Donald Davie: *New and Selected Poems* (1961)
James Dickey: *Buckdancer's Choice* (1965)
James Dickey: *Drowning With Others* (1962)
James Dickey: *Helmets* (1964)
David Ferry: *On the Way to the Island* (1960)
Robert Francis: *The Orb Weaver* (1960)
John Haines: *Winter News* (1966)
Richard Howard: *Quantities* (1962)
Barbara Howes: *Light and Dark* (1959)
David Ignatow: *Figures of the Human* (1964)
David Ignatow: *Say Pardon* (1961)
Donald Justice: *The Summer Anniversaries* (1960)
(A Lamont Poetry Selection)
Chester Kallman: *Absent and Present* (1963)
Vassar Miller: *My Bones Being Wiser* (1963)
Vassar Miller: *Wage War on Silence* (1960)
W. R. Moses: *Identities* (1965)
Donald Petersen: *The Spectral Boy* (1964)
Hyam Plutzik: *Apples from Shinar* (1959)
Vern Rutsala: *The Window* (1964)
Jon Silkin: *Poems New and Selected* (1966)
Louis Simpson: *At the End of the Open Road* (1963)
(Pulitzer Prize in Poetry, 1964)
Louis Simpson: *A Dream of Governors* (1959)
James Wright: *The Branch Will Not Break* (1963)
James Wright: *Saint Judas* (1959)